The Lives of Z

The Lives of Z

Olivia McCannon

First published 2025 by
Liverpool University Press
4 Cambridge Street
Liverpool
L69 7ZU

British Library Cataloguing-in-Publication data
A British Library CIP record is available

The manufacturer's authorised representative in the EU for product safety is:
Easy Access System Europe, Mustamäe tee 50, 10621 Tallinn, Estonia
https://easproject.com (gpsr.requests@easproject.com)

ISBN 978-1-83624-304-5 softback

Typeset by lexisbooks.com
Printed and bound in Poland by Booksfactory.co.uk

For Arthur and Imogen

Contents

Transgresser, c'est progresser
Louky Bersianik

Terra Sigillata

[medicinal earth pill]

You who are still there
you who have Z's ear
whisper all your tickling
thoughts and jokes, imaginings

to make Z smile, as zoe
collects you in, disordering
the end that you are part of,
rolling around the roles of entropy

How extrabeautiful
everything
all of you
look from here!

Z spoke this then
out of the canopy of the galaxy –

Illuminations

[Z to z]

Z's letters hang from branches
and drop onto your words

Z's pictographs are stickered on your humeholes
cubicles your chemical no-go zones

factories reactors your devices

Z's IP is all over your legalities

zoa punctuation is mutating
zoa full stops made of damaged insects

are on the move and they
are taking the page away

Celestial Questions I

[livecast | ether]

1. At the beginning of the Repro era, who was authorized to retell the story? When construct took over creation, by what means could it be scrutinised?

2. When brightness became darkness, who could fathom it? What witness remained to ask, why? How could the form of the age be recognised?

3. Who managed and measured the visible space? Who was celebrated for this achievement? Why was there a gap in the fabric of happiness?

4. When a 687-day year was found; who flocked to leave Earth? Who among them cared how broad the borders are, or where they join, or their number?

5. What divinity bore seven instruments? What eyes probed surface rock and soil? What response did the planet give? Who first looked inside the money?

6. T stands not for Time but Test. By whom was this predicted? One human deferred to another who harmed him nonetheless.

Stuck Record

[insect stutter | shellac]

Happiness is
Happiness is

a Lancet kamikaze drone a Kinzhal ballistic missile a HIMARS rocket system a Javelin anti-tank missile an L131A1 an SA80 with Flat Dark Earth coating a long-range sharpshooter with ACOG optical sight a cold-hammer-forged rifle with dimpled barrel an L-3A1 socket bayonet an Accuracy International AWM a GPMG (General Purpose Machine Gun) an M2 Browning effective range 2000 metres a counter-terrorist Remington 870 a grenade launcher red phosphorus pump action shotgun hand grenade with 15m casualty radius an M18A1 commandetonated anti-person mine an FPV a Bayraktar TB2 drone an Iskander-M ballistic

missile drone

missile drone

Swarm Model

[hume panic pattern]

A trolley dash through what is left of the world
I must deflect the knife
How will I know if I am all right

Diary Entry

[hope encrypted in DNA]

IT HAS HELPED MY
HARDENING SOFTENING HARDENING
BIOLOGICALIMAGINARYHEART TO STAY ALIVE
IN ITS SINKHOLE OF FREEZEMELTFREEZE
JUST TO HOLD MY ZLING TO SLEEP – TO SENSE
ZOA SPINE FORGIVING GRAVITY AND FLOATING
ON THE SAFETY OF PSYCHE –
AND TO BE UNBODIED DISENLARGED
BY A SUPERMASSIVE OVERSPOOLING
OF MOTHER LOVE IN A CHEMICAL MIST
BURSTING

I CAN HEAR YOUR HEART, SAID ZLING
I'M GLAD IT STILL WORKS, SAID $_{z}$I

BUT IS IT MY HEART OR IS IT THEIRS –
OF WHOSE COLLECTIVE HYPERBEING
$_{z}$I AM A DIM CONDUIT –
AGITATING ON ZLING'S BEHALF
TO MAKE ME A FUNCTION OF ZOA
SURVIVING

AS THE EXHAUSTED DISSOLVE INTO SLEEP
THEY MAKE PLANS TO WAKE AND REFORM
TOMORROW

IN DREAM $_{z}$I RADIATE ALL KINDS OF LANGUAGE
AND THE LAW IS SAYING = DOING, FIERCELY

FLICKERING DOES NOT REGISTER ON THE SPECTRUM

Zodiac in Translation I

[microseasons on the move]

GUNS, FROST

Over everything blue, still frost into sun.
Musky path, evening cows, fields of rape.
Guns stop firing, displaced pheasants roost,
drop, in everdark needlegreen plantations.

Plantation gungreens, everdropping needles,
darkspot pheasants' roosts. Fire musks
evening fields. Raped cows make paths,
sun into frost, everything over still blue.

WIRE, THISTLE

Thistle grows out of hedgerow, greening.
Farmer circles his field with barbed wire.
Plum tree, hunched, explodes blossom.
Swifts sense the lifting of light and return.

Light returns swifts, lifting, to senses.
Blossom explodes plum tree's hunch.
Barbed wire circles farmer in its field.
Greening, hedgerow outgrows thistle.

Megalith

[nucleotide-sequence repository]

In this field
where these plants and grasses and phlowers
are tipsy with being here and tall
and falling around us as we talk
shielding our eyes from the Northlight
there are suddenly walls, and bones

That they are there, is known

Layers and dead layers of leaves and creatures
picked over pits and fallen trees and excrement
of all kinds and provenances here have made
a covered humus of five thousand years
two metres deep so life is death is life
conducted earthbound in this soil

Its aftervisions aftermaths fade on
like some great guilty hidden secret

In this field there is a threshold

If you cross
you will have knowledge but no choice
the stone lines warn you not to step
where līmes is you will dissolve
you will be vague and change in there
be nothing not come back the same

You'll never find the end of seeing
only the light trapped in fog

Fable of the Firm

[pipeline-dream number-crunching]

Here be aeons
Here be millions of years
Here be gaZillions
                godzillions of
once-upon-a-time
quadrants graphs implicit costs
excess profits profiling and projections

old stories dying
with nothing beneath them but
drillions – – – krillions
= = =   o o o o oo oooo

Z's roundness is emptying out of the exits
where surfactants flood the wells
Z is awash in barrelsperday of questions
for tycoons in metric tonnes of debt to z( )e

the books don't balance there are white outs
exxes and signs where the eyes should be

+   +   +
   +   +   +
      +   +   +
         +   +   +

Road Trip Menu

[empire-infested table]

The sugar has spilled
across the map

and burned holes in it

Autoemotive Funerals

I

[zombie materialism]

The graveyards of things
are full

The places where things rest
are unrestful

Things do not know how
to say goodbye

II

[scrapyard end-rites]

when a car dies all the other cars gather round it
and honk
they want to know why it happened how it
affects them how
did it die? how does this change the way they
socially stratify?

III

[car-coffin text]

From: *The Book of Motorways*

Ah, Helpless One!
I have found you lying on your side
Did you come on the M5?

Help me out sometimehumes
I have no formula for this committal

You were more to me in your day than
crumpled metal oven-sarcophagus-fridge

You will not decay in the earth
You are corrosive cosmos-fodder
debris over ground under sky

Your petroleum spirit has arrived
at junction 3a of the M6 relief road

but your
toll has not been taken from you

IV

[final breakdown instructions]

Dig trench
Craft chamber
Raise mound
Arrange goods –

Coins ingots bowls
RAC sticker piglet bones
Candelabra carburetor
Antlers spark plugs
Fuel injector

Place
Warning triangle

Put on
Hi-vis vest
Stand well back
at side of road

Clamate on the emergency phone

Logbook

[stelliferous era wreckspeak]

The weight
Of the metals
From the car recycling plant
Has passed into my lungs
And breathing is now a
Sinking

The fluorohydrocarbons
Leaking out of
The fridge cemetery
Are debilitating
My capacity for
Ecstasy

The over-permanence
Of the plastics
That flip around my ankles
Prevents me from embracing
The playfulness of
Wind

My present cannot
Love my past
As beauty when
The future reads it
Backwards into
Power

Celestial Questions II

[livecast | ether]

1. Orbital velocity of 17,500mph is reached in 8.5 minutes. What is the limit of speed?

2. Fuel tank capacity is 383,000 gallons of hydrogen and 143,000 gallons of liquid oxygen. Why do three dimensions feel more spacious than two?

3. Past microbial life forms clusters, fossils can be mapped. Where is the place of immortality?

4. Molecules have a spectral fingerprint; light scatters, luminescent. What knows to what purpose?

5. Why did the efficient son kill his mother, so that her petrified corpse burst open on the ground? Who threw the camera out of the hatch?

6. Gases escape the atmosphere into space; what makes the wind stir? Why does matter want to be conscious?

Decomposition

[riddled paper]

Silverfish ate book. Leaving   holes for words to
wrap. Important hume names   were on this book, for
years protected as forcibly   inherited property
from thieves-in-the-night, moorless brigands   etc
though the damp got in easily.   Now, between   sheets –
a house-mate   immune to any locking   and
bolting of doors   of hanging rowan   charms
from blackened beams, or hooking up security to
buzz mole operatives on the under-lawn approach.
The book   grew a culture of forgetting   became the
bright forgottenness of funghi   while the silverfish
were thorough, paying   attention
seemingly of the   wrong kind
though why not   put those
sometimehume words   to good re-
creational use? How else to change what appears
to be written   to digest words differently
remake the dotted line in motion
to bed down in the page   make it matter
to eat nest reproduce

Lexical Waste Deposit

[metaphor | carbon black | cellulose]

First iteration | anthropocentric

Z –

Blossom of my heart
Lichen of my lungs
Rootball of my womb
Acritarch of my unconscious

Second iteration | parasitic

Z –

Plasmodium of my blood of my mosquitoes
Trichinosis of my intestine of my roundworms
Mansonellosis of my skin of my blackflies

Third iteration | symbiotic

Z –

flower of my	tongue tongue	of my flower
seed of my	fur fur	of my seed
pollen of my	muzzle muzzle	of my pollen
nectar of my	wings wings	of my nectar
blossom of my	bat bat	of my blossom

Pod

[cœur de la mer]

Here is closed and lonely, zlings
Throw me a thoughtsound – drift it
from elsewhere, copteric seed

I want a growchange word
to make the time-space-
shape of liberty

Scroll

[squid ink on talipat leaf]

0.0000001 Z was born walked six steps forwards and at each
step an island appeared in zoa cosmic ocean
0.0001 Z laughed zoa breath was wet and warm zoa spit fell
as rain and flourished the plants and trees
0.01 Z shook zoa hair so swarms of insects flew out bright and
loud their carapaces shining blue and green
01 Spiders shot out on dragline silk to weave from a pattern
respooling and never completing
10 Birds hurtled up and out low high to hear and be heard sing
and be sung to be the lungs of the sky
100 Z heard how the old earth longed to howl and wept along with
its rocks so blood lava salt flowed into lakes
1100 Z went on five journeys met a sick being an old being
the bones of a being and a being-becoming
10100 Z existed ∞ in rocks in gases in aquifers ferns in
dragonflies in dying stars in plankton
1001000 Wherever Z walked zoa footprints filled with crude oil
and were dogged by hume time and design
1000100000 Z's auspicious emblem is infinity accommodating any
thing orangeslice umbrella goldfish daisy
snailshell piggybank
protestbanner
lithium
sunlight
lead

Z Z Z Z Z
Z Z Z Z

Cyclopean Tube

[debris cloud | rainbands]

category phenomena are in
thing of process creature
of speech of being of
$_{z}$I $_{z}$we $_{z}$they all parts
warm   air $_{z}$you
rising   is   the
rising   this
warm air
is   the
this

Zodiac in Translation II

[microseasons on the move]

DRONE, TICK

Bursting pods tick in rising grass on banks.
Bee-drone drops. Beetles burrow bark. Sun
reddens river. Peaks of measured furrows
flush green. Clouds scatter light in heat.

Heat cracks dry furrows. Storm parts banks,
rivers rise and peak. Redds break up, drones
measure. In grass, flesh-ticks burrow, drop.
Bark rots, spores disperse, scatter in clouds.

DOG, REEDS

Reeds form unread letters in the marsh –
mirror of wild geese turning. Supertide
shifts ocean over land, deserts dogfish,
beaches carton, rope twist, and the moon.

Mirror-moon twists on marsh eel rope, in
sky geese have deserted. Tide is turning,
superscented by dog, as fish. Beach, ocean
reform, carton shifts, blows into reeds.

Pass Word

[encrypted system hack]

$_{z}$I am searching through unsafe words
for charms that will bear my weight my
hume-made mass my impure places

Document fans replace my hands
and whatever it was I thought I was making

welcome qwerty admin mixeddelphinium
iloveyousunshine shadow RememberMe?

Where do $_{z}$I want to go? If pushed,
to the land of the deadly and back again

having forgotten all the shortcuts
sensing this as ending this as beginning

poised with polymesmerising wand
to scramble nameless agents of control

to unsubscribe Z's shimmering field of
being from what's left of knowing

with no reason at all to keep agreeing

Landmark Definition

[high-level indexrisk exposure]

The markets are not immune to epidemic
their process is insentient but
transoceanic virus makes
their pulse space out
their pressure drop they pale
and crumple when the factories close
when nothing works and nothing moves
as winds blow global webs to holes

is this the brake
the one the system didn't make

Ice Core Specimen

[insulated sample tube]

The Dow Jones is melting

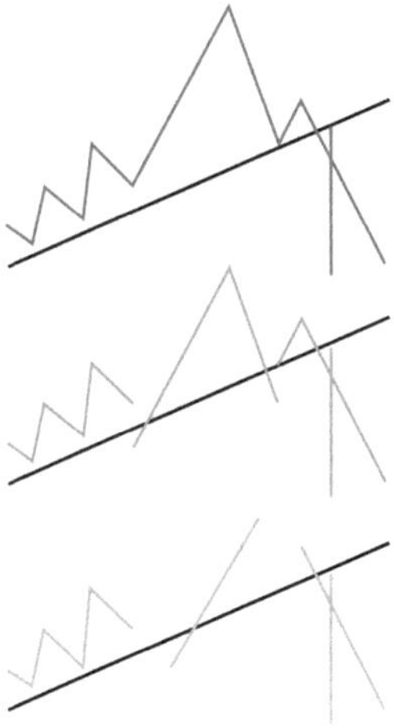

Celestial Questions III

[livecast | ether]

1. 42,000 satellites launched in low earth orbit; many break down. Which bodies catch the fragments of debris?

2. Anyone is able, I am able to do what I want. If money is no object, by what method can this be proved wrong?

3. Everything can be seen with a strong enough lens. How does a microscope reveal morality?

4. When Entrepreneur E moved to Mars, what made the people willing to follow him? What warning was issued?

5. How did the chickens recognise the butcher? He was humming and sharpening knives; why was he so happy?

6. When the Federal Commission gave the mandate, what human granted another human permission to grant another human ownership of heaven?

Usnea Capture

[exoplanetologist flitthought]

In these fizzing grey nights
when I scopescan the sky
I have lost my antique sense
of whether that weakbright
is the round hope of Ross 128b
or Gliese 667 or Trappist 1

or the aborted hotrock of Mars
or the latest salvagefix of the ISS
collecting eternity's data in LEO
or a shower of debris degrading
to fastflash in graveyard orbit
massbatteryimpactexplosions but

I do keep revisioning the sky
still look up, and out, into that
flow and fill with the strange
warm awe of sentience –
I trust the story yes I'm
searching for some luck

some old-sun slant glint
heatsigning that sweetdark
whose spiralling spins safe
the matter of Z, reworking
here-life in the helices of
what was everywhere.

Oracle Bone Script

[unfree radicals]

many are watching for the breaking points
of bubbles the shifting magnetic field
in the pigeon's beak

Spectogram

[skyprint]

Caught it! Vulture as you're staying Z will use your moulted feather as a quill to rewrite in the space of flight or as a hook to unpick chains dissociate each dying loop and make new endocrine reports unfastened from the neurotoxins jamming Z's migration patterns seizing up zoa small-winged swarms and zoa granivorous gleaners of mosaic-fire-desiring seeds – speargrass sorghum schizachyrium scattered gone

Z hereby unnames firebirds
Temmincks   Courser
Gouldian Finch
Golden-shouldered parrot
Carpentarian Grasswren
Demon duck
Z recalls you in zoa molecular clouds
Firehawk you will stay
until there's nothing more
to burn or chase
Z hereby unnames forestbirds
Spix's macaw
Alagoas foliage-gleaner
Pernambuco pygmy-owl
Rio Branco antbird
Hoary-throated spinetail

Z recalls you in zoa active galactic nuclei
Z's co-signatories of sky   exultant birds   for now there's nothing left to see here but   uncoupled hume-words   circled names   not given to   but   taken from   still   know the overunderstory   will go on   signed   Z

Aircon Residue

[Legionella colony]

honey you don't need to worry
everywhere we go we are
looking for a coat for you

he wasn't happy
with the restaurant so
I said you choose
where we eat
tonight

what now
want me to call the car?

time is after lunch before dinner

I should get a new watch
this one's stuck on old

why is it so warm in here?

we can make it cooler see like this

Postcard

[drift litter]

The ANTIQUES sign in the saguaro's desert –
dirtbrass Old West font on blackmesh trailer
with meltscraped mountains behind –

is tailed by an alley of short black stakes,
started letters missing tendrils, nearly-writing
the track from nowhere to nowhere else

The tufts of scrub, the scraggy stripbark bushes
whatevertheirnamesare will always be
zcellves, wrestling with intruders here

in Z's own space where tumbleweed tropes
show all the shifting ways to go, bowling
and snagging in the pushblow of wind's voice

There are no landmarks and tall names grow rust
on a cage that once held high-end trash | the past
is mountain bush and sign is paradigm of dust

Canalisation

[rerouted dreamscape]

channel that can or can't
change course of history
water diverted to close over
what is adjacent to mud

*must promote
global supply*

meanwhile
there's a little song $_{z}$I wish
to still be allowed to hum
to be hume

a little meandering tune
taking me out with my questions
into the open breathable air

where the morning glory
tendrils out of Z's heads
and zoa hands flow waters

Letter

[surface debris]

Dear Editors-of-Creation,

The Z within I send you these archives from your future's past which is your being present in perpetuity.

Filed by agents hume-ingened to harvest intel here you find the trace of who you were and where how what became.

They reconjig your tech, mutate your tongues, your concepts, disalign your systems, redesign your misbeliefs and stories, are bulletproof but harmless unlike you, and yet

they have no insense kin with matter – magnetics – no pheromones hormones – lack all roots for feeling entropy – dimension time space place. It's funny how confusedly

they speak your Science. Its case is never closed and they want answers but despite themselves make one unspooling song of love-destruction, synched to Z.

zI send you these to ask if you will play Z's game. Z has infiltered all the data, left zoa prints on every thought and thing, signed them with Z's names.

Sincerely,

Beast Bank

[memrefacts]

Z6P5–129

sweet zling my youngling
smiling surface into relief

sweet beloved sweetness
blossom of Z's old heart
zoa poor knackered crust

let Z watch you forever
becoming peacock
opening out into grandeur

rattling forth strong-
shouldered with a flick
your boned dome-fan

turning your circular dance
shaking the feathers of your making parts
shapesounding peacock paon
                                        paon paon

sweetness of Z's making earth
spoken to speaking back

Z3R8–863

Z's mind is rabbit
today and probably always
young rabbit found in the road
on its side with the beak-open sky
shrieking in its eye
whole-body shaking
with the terror of
pain never ending again

Z will remake you
a dark place
of shelter, away
in the woods
where sheep come to die
leaving their skulls behind

In the red bank
soil a chthonic hole
for the roundness of your
soft begun body
for the continuing of your beginning of your end
and its continuing

Z will seal your receded eyes with small
reopening suns – dandelion primrose
Rabbit in the woods
your absence presence paraconsistent
in Z's always-mind

ZIWI–000

The entire ocean changes for a single whale
Ocean's purpose is emptied without whales
Ocean turns in listless raging cycles, lacking
Z's translations, endless, zoa vast returners
zoa four-thousand-mile filterers, hydro-
singers, making the epic song of dimensions
ring low dark through bones or breakboom
through distance accounted in plankton   Z will
drift your snow down deep o whales   will
bury you in Zcellf & gyre you over to secretive
bubblers, microsifters of biotreasure who'll
mesh you with raspings you never you again

Z7S4–691

Exalted August Slugs –
your private dance
co-coiling in full solar
on Z's given path
your white nebulae
secretions
shimmer
life's plans

Zodiac in Translation III

[microseasons on the move]

EGGS, NETS

So little matters. Sensing matters.
Floodrushsliprhythmshadowpulse
feeding matters. Tumbling in tide-rip
networked flanks light with shudders.

Nets lit up by plankton, rip.
Slipping launce, tuna, purse-seine,
matters. Broadcasting egg-zillions into
ebb-flood, matters. Little life works.

CORAL, BLOOM

Eyespots scope crevices, acoustic fat and
bone map prawnsnap and pincer-click. Jelly
spawn, pheromones shout. Zooxanthellae
feed the reef, coral colours. Water warms.

"   ". Corals spit zoozanthellae and
starve. Shells dissolve, skeletons implode.
'   '. Silence is a falling into algae bloom.
Jellies shape water, spots of colour, feeding.

Still Life Report

[Point Nemo stream]

gyre & there's not much to eat
round here

cold into hot
hot into cold

what does it mean to be
no where?

what is the sound that sings
no body?

Seashipburialsite

[pingchirpboom detection | sand backscatter]

∞ ∞
∞
∞ ∞
∞
∞ ∞
∞ ∞ ∞
∞ ∞ ∞

∞ remember I lovedlived did wrong
∞ as well as right as well as any thing ∞

∞ my signatures are sacs of water any where ∞
∞ my imprints   cirrus sand clouds
my shoes are full of soil of blooming excrement trails
my pockets   of waving plastic fronds ∞

∞
∞ here are my unconditional leavings ∞
∞ here are my organic-synthetic materials ∞
∞ cucumber bristleworm hagfish sleepershark ∞
∞ are you there? cleave to my parts consume my whole

∞ ∞
welcome dear agents of deepwater decomposition ∞
keep me from the longcoldfear of hydrostatic preservation

Celestial Questions IV

[livecast | ether]

1. Advisor A hanged himself in the hotel. What was the reason for this? Who did this frighten?

2. President P fled to his outpost; dined on pheasant. How did he exist for so long?

3. General G hid away in a cave. How could his predicament be reported?

4. Commissioner C was not afraid to return. Why? What was she seeking?

5. What did the respondent draw on the ground? How did the transformation occur?

6. What was it that M managed? What was it that K completed?

Transparency Chart

[laminated lie reflector]

T R U T H

S I G H T

P L A I N

Y E A H

R I G H T

Mutoptopia

[fire evacuation plan]

zWe are living in a State
that is delusional

No-place-else-to-go is on the
first floor with the hyperreal,

randomly animated vistas
made of prison squares and

technospherebiosphere fuzz-
glitch   In the basement,

sanctuary is both well-
equipped and imaginary

reforming the characters
of the letters above the gate

S o m e w h e r e

in Z's heretheredom
the dying converse with

the unborn in water where
they hear each other speak

Sample

[tropospheric microbiome]

z How old are you mother?

Z Fourteen billion in the ether. And you, little one?

z I'm four point five billion in the water.

Z And how big have you been all this time?

z ∞

Ziggurat

[necrodialogue]

Is this my code word my high place
my hiding space my priest hole
my shrine my administrative heart?

The water is rising

Is this my safety? The path left mined
the craters deep the air napalmed
the walls shot through with shells?

The water is rising

Is this my future? Z re-
fuses

Z will reuse the use
Review the view

The moon waxes then wanes
Then waxes again

Some of the creatures on the floodplains
swim up to the light

Boundary Stone

[earthquake-exposed concrete]

I AM WHAT YOU WILL NOT KEEP I
HAVE NO EDGES IF YOU DRAW ME
DRAW ME INSIDE OUT OR OUTSIDE
IN I AM BECOMING WHAT UNDID I
WAS NOT WHAT I WILL BE LET ME
PASS UNSEEN I SWIM THE RIVER
HAVE NO CLOTHES NO SHOES NO
PAPERS WHAT HAVE YOU DONE
WITH MY LIFE I WANT IT BACK

Grave Tin

[spoilheap methane exhalation]

I have been waiting for so long to speak
to revoice backleak dissonance again.
My scream has hung unended for somany a
stardeath, meteorbloom reseeding, since
my lungs expelled all radiant air and cleaned
themselves so that I'd be for then complete –
My new life was becoming – you who find me
you will chart its place here, trace and draw
the mesh I was becoming as you look.
You who know I see it who can feel that
I-in-pieces am still hume, if that means
z-who-rots, zoa story gone to earth,

rebreathing with zoa great bacteria lungs –

work me out. Although displaced my voice
sounds isotopic time in bonedeep space,
age in my not-yet-fused bones, their flakes
leprotic breaks and broad sciatic notch,
the oddslant wear of my teeth and here close by
my disarticulated child – hard-born
weight of my fibula, bulrush of my pond,
bulge of my stem, companion of renewal,
of spent cells, huge abscess of my pain,
cuts of my grief. Translate this pit –
Note well what I once ate, what I remade
with my bedfellow, Z, multizoan in the soil

Midden

[landfill gas pocket]

| o |

The	*t*	urtles	elephones	ailbacks
	h	overflies	elicopters	ailstones
	i	ntroverts	guanas	mperialists
	n	enuphars	anopods	ettles
	g	orillas	oblins	host crabs
	s	nakes	ausages	ousentendus

signified

should be valued more than their signs

– Augustine –

o | o

$_{z}$I am writing from the space that is left
The crack between my label and my name
Will this sprinkle of soil darkness light rain
Be strong enough to vivify the cleft – ?

Solstice Lozenge

[citizen misrule decree]

Z is changing zoa channels
days are longer in a slow spin

midgard is just scaffolding
with limitless free slots

for listening to
the terribly tangled stories

collecting in the heartwood
where the regrowth begins

Zodiac in Translation IV

[microseasons on the move]

FLOOD, FLAKES

Poultry fill the land, crated on planes in time
for floods of fake snowflakes and white beards.
Plastic sheets are removed before heating. Hume-
fossils turn up ancient Rock. Ice cubes clink.

Rain follows snow, heated sheets of whitemelt
flood, after-ice plains turn up fossil
poultry, landfill. Unremoved in hume-
time, plastic flakes, fuses with rock, craters.

MOOSE, MOSS

Lakes vanishing, tundra. The earth spins faster.
Permafrost is also a memory of fish. Tussak grass,
blueberry, lichen, moss. Dark plants suck in sun,
moose crop where shrubs stick up through snow.

Snow – ever snow, never snow. White mousse,
winter's moss. Tussocks are new, and sable. Fish
were old. Faster, vanishing faster. The tundra spins,
tossed for. Memory is also the sun sucking up lakes.

Tablet

[blankscreen mindtap]

Twelve mines exploding
Eleven windows smashing
Ten fridges leaking
Nine wildfires spreading
Eight levees flooding
Seven swans a-singing
Six cells mutating
Five plastic bins
Four silenced birds
Three lost bees
Two latex gloves
and a cartridge in a bare tree

Softwear Manual

[late-hume first-aid kit]

popping with sound of seedbod bursting
A was wearing the pill on the inside

had swallowed a friend of the narcocartel
was full of hopes and fatalities and dreams

of complex protohume feelings with no
place in the blister-pack promise of shine

B said let there be bankable sadness and
pain in the parasomniac lives of cyborgs

let there be rows of small white cupboards
for weltering hearts   proferring keys

inviting clicks within the clearnet £*!
putting the patent first
                                        Z zig-zags away

turns whirling being in the garden of dusk
ecstasy in motion in the birdsung light

Celestial Questions V

[livecast | ether]

1. The rover blasts into the air. Why are humans less free than the rover? Whose translation is this, why is it given no name?

2. What were the tiles made of? How were they attached? In whose backyard did the bird shed its feathers?

3. Children are handed the questionnaire by their parents; who is tasked with knowing, who with discovering?

4. Minister M was incapable of controlling the flood; why did the masses revere him? The crevasse was deep; how did he fill it?

5. What shook the forest of stones? How did the wrong head fall by mistake? How did injustice become a carpet to walk on?

6. Who claims to own the matter of life? Death: why is it claimed in other names? Whom does the mandate of heaven punish, whom protect?

Simcard

[memory shards]

sun winter tents low few small-ones
litter dirt play woods stop night

sky star clear all-ones fire red
pot drink home phone family look

van siren blue flash state come
beat tall-ones crack screen stamp fire

nappy leaflet map ticket train no
alone crossing smash centre wound mind

few small-ones walk feet west bare
run lorry absence wind empty hope

Birdsight

[postharvest migration]

sunrise

flying low over the gouged earth
dragged bare herbicidal matter
cracking between rows no weeds

sundown

searching for seeds beetles closed
ears of wheat fallen across the
dipping sightline of ${}_{z}$us flying low

sunup

over the hinterharvest bodies of
need shadowhosts crossing striated
soil calling searching as wind

sunset

counters direction reorders straw
mid-air no trees storm vents ${}_{z}$us
ex horizon backwards turning

Thermal View from the Pont au Change

[aerial drone erasures]

Conciergerie	stone, cold
Cargo ship	coal, metal, cold
Sainte Chapelle	stone, cold
~~Bridgesitter hume (f)~~	~~flesh, cool~~
Musée du Louvre	stone, cold
Tuileries	stone, cold
Leisureboathumes (mf pl)	flesh, warm
~~Sleepingbag humes (mf pl)~~	~~flesh, cool~~
Musée d'Orsay	stone, cold
Obélisque Place de la Concorde	stone, cold
Cargo ship	ore, metal, cold
Petit Palais	stone, cold
Grand Palais	stone, cold
~~Legdragging hume (f)~~	~~flesh, hot~~
Palais de Tokyo	stone, cold
Container ship	cars, metal, cold
Tour Eiffel	metal, cold
~~Pavementlying hume (m)~~	~~flesh, cold~~

Chalice

[bloody instructions]

Labels Loss
Captions Cruelty
Rituals Power
Epigrams Horror
Slogans Desire
Definitions Faith
Subdivisions Fear
Empty shells Belief
Signs Paranoia
Epitaphs Grief
Spells Despair
Formulae Comfort
Abbreviations Denial
Warnings Love
Riddles Hope

Celestial Questions VI

[livecast | ether]

1. The elders possessed the Dead Mound. Why did the younger ones desire it? How did the birds lose their bodies?

2. Who sowed black seed, and exploited the rushes and reeds? What caused them to modify?

3. Who sought the wonder cure they could not safely conceal? Where did they get it?

4. How many were the military? Who did Opponent O offend, so that he was eradicated?

5. Why did Agent A go in pursuit of him. But end up poisoning the child? Who invented the information?

6. Encountering the errors of zoa codecessors, Z's multibeing corrected them. What more is to be said?

Fragment

[birch bark]

On that nonspecific day of war to end all war | lungs split by the holy father of all bombs
Z shuts zoa three bright eyes | of sun moon fire and signals
understorywise to six-leg crits | to reinvest the emptied space
bees arachnids hornets flesh flies | termites beetles wasps mosquitoes
coat zoa corporeal crust | together-acting, crawl zoa limbs
zoa skin zoa hair zoa eyelids | black wave dark dirge breaking
over ruins on battle wastes | to click at scars recontour
ragged tabs of scorched | of deep-gouged earthflesh
Antleg tickled, hydrocarbon | washed, Z revels, smiling out
zoa radiance, makes rifts | revealing corridors of coming into being
It was all over by evening

Spindroin Patch

[ghost data]

Somewhere between
thin branches is
the spider, spinning hider

mind, maker
springing strings that
sing its purpose into holder

form. Look how when
the spider's gone
the web remains
hunger

Votive Offerings

[synthetic fossils]

$_z$I And what do you want for your birthday?

zling I want there to be fish. and cougars.
and congers. and plankton.
and a fruit bat with a sugared nose.

For there to be cranes. and sunstars.
rhinos. and a million kinds
of creatures with no bones.

I want there to be you and I.
and us. I want there to be Z.
I want to never be alone.

Acknowledgements

This book owes its making to many extraordinary humes.

The 'Z' project emerged from an AHRC-funded creative practice Ph.D. at Newcastle University, through the boundless support and inspiration of Sinéad Morrissey, Tara Bergin and Pauline Henry-Tierney. I am also grateful to Bill Herbert, Michael Rossington and a host of researchers and staff I long for the space to list here.

My heartfelt thanks for all kinds of vital Z-related conversations and encounters are due to Jamie, Arthur and Imogen, Sasha Dugdale, Bernhard Malkmus, Linda France, Karen Leeder and Tessi Loeffelmann.

I wish to particularly acknowledge the skilled and sensitive typesetting design by J.O. Morgan that brought Z to life on the page.

'Scroll' and 'Letter,' 'Megalith' and 'Boundary Stone' first appeared in *Shearsman* and *Dark Mountain* respectively. 'Boundary Stone' was translated into Flemish by Alicja Gescinska for DW *B*. Thank you to the editors of these magazines.

I owe a huge debt of gratitude to Alison Welsby and to all those who worked on this book at Pavilion Poetry and LUP. Thank you, finally, to Deryn Rees-Jones, without whose leap of faith and nurturing vision this book would not exist.

Notes

What is Z? A translator multibeing, a plural persona, an open experiment.

These poems are beginners, curious, wanting to learn all the languages in which I-human will never be fluent. They are attempts to read, as much as write, an unreadable world.

The poems work through all kinds of responses to 'Anthropocene Horror' (Timothy Clark). Fear has a paralysing effect. For the work to be constructive, it needed to move, and breathe.

I wanted the experimentation of Z to be fearless, for Z to be free to write anything. Z responded with the tangled irreverence of the spoilheap, where nothing is stable, or stands alone, or is pure.

Who or what is speaking? Everybeing and all times at once, layering, nesting and overunderwriting. Biosphere and technosphere simultaneously.

A creative energy is at work, processing material and ethereal human debris. Belonging as much to a speculative 'future past' as to an overlooked 'future present': a present with tangible futures nested within it.

Each poem is written with and grown from elsewhere: from the centres of works in all kinds of media; from conversations and encounters with living and technological forms, human and beyond, across place and time.

Occasionally the poems assert a right to roam through material that is sacred to some humans. Not to appropriate, or exploit, or destroy, but much as a weed makes free within a graveyard where there is soil and a patch of sun. They are hungry for unofficial wildernesses.

The out-of-reach ambition of these poems was to be exhaustively inexhaustible, bound up with the complexity of connected being. They are messily networked and incomplete.

The 'notes' below are selective. There are countless other strands sticking out of the text for you to pick up and play with, if you wish.

Z & ...

Louky Bersianik: Québécoise writer, poet and (eco)feminist (1930–2011) and the originator in French of 'the feminisation of language, a revolutionary invention of considerable symbolic importance' (France Théoret).

Terra Sigillata: 'Terra sigillata,' or 'stamped earth,' refers to clay believed to have medicinal properties, usually made into cakes or tablets and authenticated with a stamp. First used circa 500 BCE on the island of Lemnos, in Greece.

zoe (first appearing in **'Terra Sigillata'**): An experiment. What if there was a 'multibeing' pronoun in English, accommodating assemblages of human, nonhuman and more-than-human existence? What if English had a 'collective possessive' pronoun, to counter delusions of individual ownership of Earth?

Emboldened by Louky Bersianik's feminising inventions (see above) and Rosie Braidotti's 'Four Theses on Posthuman Feminism' (2017), $_{z}$I 'coined' Z's 'personal' and 'possessive' collective pronouns – *zoe* and *zoa* – by propagating an older Greek word for life: *zoë*.

The mini zs periodically attached to 'I,' 'you,' 'we,' 'they,' gesture towards the instability of a human considered to be e.g. 57% microbe, 40% cyborg etc. $_{z}$I was picturing the subscripted atomic numbers of the periodic table.

Illuminations: Medieval monks would spend years illuminating manuscripts made of animal skins, leaving their acne or other bacteria lodged in the material (molecular data for biochemists).

What is a page made of? What else lives there apart from words? If the book is left open, what kinds of life can escape from the print?

Celestial Questions I: The first of six 'Questions' poems, scattered through the sequence, responding to translations by

David Hawkes and others of *Tianwen* ('Heavenly Questions'): the Chinese (Warring States period) poem by Qu Yuan (340–278 BCE), for which the 2021 Republic of China Mars Mission spacecraft (Tianwen-1) was named.

Stuck Record: John Lennon took the title of his collaged Beatles song 'Happiness is a Warm Gun' from the cover of a 1968 issue of *American Rifleman*. War then, war now.

Swarm Model: 'Hume' is a human imagined closer to humus: '… a microbiome of fermenting critters of many genders and kinds i.e. companion species, at table together, eating and being eaten, messmates, compost.' (Donna Haraway, *Staying with the Trouble*, 2016).

Zodiac in Translation I: The first of four Zodiac poems, scattered throughout the sequence, responding to:

The concept of the microseason, from the traditional Japanese almanac, which invites attentiveness to small but significant transformations marking the cyclical translations of Earth. What other microseasons might now refigure calendar years?

Joyelle McSweeney, writing, 'Just as this catastrophe consists of microactions, poems may radiate their effects on microscales,' in 'Every poem an Escrache' (2015).

Michèle Métail's translations and commentaries of Chinese reversible poetry (third to nineteenth century) in *Le vol des oies sauvages* (Tarabuste, 2011).

The multi-directional migrations and returns of the wild geese of her title, the form and the content of the poems, the relationships they (re)make between time, place and subjects, suggest a tongue of shifting and shared agency.

Megalith: Rows of standing stones at Carnac in Brittany. Olafur Eliasson's fog tunnel at Tate Modern (2019).

This poem, and 'Grave Tin,' exist because of Dr Tessi Loeffelmann (Durham University), who gave up valuable time to explain how an archaeologist thinks, and what she does, both in the archives and in the field at a dig.

Autoemotive Funerals: learning and translating as a beginner, for example:

II From descriptions of the social behaviour of the Australian magpie (a bird that doesn't hoard or thieve but displays altruistic behaviours i.e. does things to help others of its species in distress which will bring it no direct benefit).

III From the rituals and spells of the Ancient Egyptian Pyramid Texts. With wonder, and a desire for more meaning than motorways can give to existence.

IV From Viking ship burials. How to bid cars farewell.

Decomposition: Imagining kin to ghosts and beasts of Riddle 47 in the Exeter Manuscript. Not to scale.

Lexical Waste Deposit: An experiment with rethinking the structure of metaphor. Responding to 'Ladders, Trees, Complexity, and Other Metaphors in Evolutionary Thinking,' by Andreas Hejnol, in *Arts of Living on a Damaged Planet* (2018).

Pod [*cœur de la mer*]: a Caribbean seedpod that disperses across vast distances and continents via Earth's rivers and oceans, and contains an air pocket.

'The thinking of wandering releases the imagination, projects us far from that imprisoning cave in which we were huddled, which is the hold or the rock of [...] so-called powerful uniqueness'

(Édouard Glissant tr. Betsy Wing, *Treatise on the Whole-World,* 2020)

Pass Word: The words in italics feature in online lists of common (often hacked) passwords.

Usnea Capture: ISS, International Space Station. LEO, Low Earth Orbit. Usnea is a bearded lichen which scientists have found will survive in simulated Mars conditions. Imagined here recording future-past traces of a human exoplanetologist's musings.

Plant sentience: Emmanuele Coccia *The Life of Plants* (2018), Ursula K. Le Guin *The Word for World is Forest* (1976), Richard Powers *The Overstory* (2018).

Spectogram: Juliana Spahr's *Well then there now* (2011), Ursula K. Heise's *Imagining Extinction* (2016).

Aircon Residue: 'Watches are things that humans read. But they are also things that flies land on, things that lizards ignore, things that the sun glints off.' Timothy Morton, *Being Ecological* (2018).

Postcard: Antiques sign photographed by Barry Cawston, in his series 'An American Road Trip' (viewed 2020).

Rights of Nature: 'Saguaro, Free of the Earth,' Boyce Upholt, *Emergence* magazine (2022).

Seashipburialsite: 'Voices from the Deep' (2018) exhibition at the Postal Museum in London, displaying letters and everyday objects that sank with *SS Gairsoppa* on 16 February 1941.

Transparency Chart: David James Duncan's *Sun House,* Chapter VI: 'On Irony (*Yeah, Right*),' provides an antidote.

Ziggurat: Vast moon temples built by the Sumerians from 4000 BCE. Liable to become islands during violent seasonal flooding of the Tigris and Euphrates. Epic of Gilgamesh.

Boundary Stone: Inscribed in the time of 'Trump's Wall.' Etruscan boundary stones marked personal connection with a plot of land.

Midden: Quotation attributed to St Augustine, gleaned once then lost forever due to pandemic disorder.

Softwear Manual: Artist and activist Jenni Dutton makes dresses from salvage, including one from empty pill packets.

Simcard: Modelled on a translational form adapted from *Awakened Cosmos*, by David Hinton (2019) and exploring his comment that 'English grammar contains no wildness.'

Fragment: Given momentum by a fleeting encounter with myths of the Hindu goddess of black bees, Bhrāmarī.